T0105556

Short Stories

for

Short Flights

Short Stories

for

Short Flights

Maurice P. Sullivan

Order this book online at www.trafford.com
or email orders@trafford.com

Most Trafford titles are also available at major online book retailers.

Printed in the United States of America.

ISBN: 978-1-4269-0759-3 (sc)
ISBN: 978-1-4269-7866-1 (e)

Trafford rev. 05/24/2012

 www.trafford.com

North America & international
toll-free: 1 888 232 4444 (USA & Canada)
phone: 250 383 6864 ◆ fax: 812 355 4082

To all those excited by the sound of a plane,

The smell of aviation exhaust fumes,

And the sensation of banking into a turn.

Table of Contents

Preface

The stories in this book all have an aviation theme but they were not written for pilots. Only two tenths, of one percent, of the United States population holds a pilot's license, but a large number of people have a deep interest in aviation. They subscribe to flying magazines, attend air shows by the thousands, and take flights in restored World War II aircraft. Some go out of their way to find restaurants at small airfields so they can watch planes take off and land while having dinner. Many purposely sit in the cramped window seat of an airliner so they can watch and hear the leading edge slats, flaps, and spoilers deploy and retract.

Countless people dream of learning to fly, but don't. Maybe it's because of the expense, or the time demands of their families and careers. However, those who dream of flying share something with the aviators they envy: an appreciation and awe of the machines that can carry them to distant places and, sometimes, even to adventure. Such people will enjoy these stories. As a side benefit, the stories may help sustain their interest until they too decide to climb into the cockpit, start the engine, and feel the thrill of guiding a plane down the runway and toward the clouds.

Split Decision

A light summer drizzle fell on the yellow convertible sliding to a stop at the airline terminal building. Jack Wilson sat motionless staring out the window. The bright lights reflecting from his face and dark hair gave him a mannequin-like appearance. "Jack, Jack!" He jumped reflexively and looked at his wife.

"Sorry, guess I was thinking." Actually, he had been daydreaming. Jack had always been a daydreamer but lately he had been doing it more often.

"Sometimes, Jack, you live in a different world."

"Could be," he laughed, leaning over for a kiss. Barbara placed a finger on his nose and stopped his face inches from her own. She knew he was a dreamer. Jack was a just-like-the-movies pilot who had little interest in anything but flying. Their two girls were in high school, and Jack Jr. would be a sophomore at Dawson College in the fall. Overnight flights and weather delays had caused Jack's family to miss him often. Barbara felt his time away from home had prevented him from really knowing the kids.

"Lately, you've been more distant than usual."

"Yeah. Something's bothering me, but I don't know what." Barbara was smiling. Jack considered her smile unique: slight parting of the lips; a subdued wildness in her eyes. "How about a trip to Laurel Mountain this weekend?"

"I'd love to, but we can't. Julie has a dance coming up, the school's open house is next week, and...."

"Okay, okay, forget it. We'll make it another time." They kissed and he pushed his lanky frame out of the car just as it started to rain. Leaning back into the car he reminded Barbara to stop at a gas station.

"Don't worry, I'm used to you leaving me an

empty tank. I need to stop at the mall to pick up some stuff for Julie anyway".

Jack's philosophy was that he should optimize his time at home. Time spent pumping gas was less time spent with Barbara. He watched the convertible melt into the traffic as he ran toward the terminal. He strode quickly through the chaos of hustling people, oblivious to the activity surrounding him. He weaved his way through porters tugging luggage carts, late travelers rushing for planes, and winding lines of people pushing to buy tickets.

"Excuse me," Jack said elbowing his way through a stationary mass of people. He felt he really needed some time away with Barbara. Kids. They sure make a marriage difficult, he thought. He and Barbara often took spontaneous trips when the kids were younger. Now their whole life seemed to revolve around ball games, overnight parties and a thousand other functions he couldn't begin to keep track of. "Oh well," he muttered as he entered the Seneca Airlines flight office, "you owe kids something."

"Hi, Captain." Mike Davis rushed up to Jack at the flight desk. He was one of Seneca's newest pilots. "Already have the weather. We'll lose this rain thirty miles out and have good visibility at both stops. Want to look this over?" Mike shoved a clipboard into Jack's hand.

He quickly checked the flight plan, cargo list, and other information. Mike was conscientious and, as usual, he had already pre-flighted the plane. His freckled face and slight build made him appear younger than his twenty-four years. Jack classified this co-pilot with the new breed. Mike had only been flying commercial for two years and, unlike Jack, had no military flying experience. He considered the younger fellows different. Oh, they were capable, but they were different.

"Let's go." Jack returned the clipboard and headed for the door. They ran the few feet to the boarding stairs and entered the cabin just as the drizzle became a heavy rain.

"Hello, Jack, Mike." Amy Dennis hurriedly greeted them. Jack was glad to have Amy managing the cabin crew. Her demeanor and ability guaranteed no passenger complaints. "Which of you guys brought the rain?"

"Blame me," Mike laughed, "my tomatoes were dry."

Jack stepped into the cockpit and slipped into the left seat. The narrow cockpit windows framed activity all about the plane. He watched a fuel truck pull away as a baggage train disappeared under the fuselage. The reflected light patterns of blinking aircraft lamps, vehicle headlights and the glow from the terminal windows created a constantly changing kaleidoscopic effect on the wet concrete.

So he raises tomatoes, Jack thought to himself. The new guys definitely were different. Not that he saw anything wrong with raising tomatoes; he just didn't know why anyone enjoyed raising tomatoes. The day after graduating from college he had joined the Air Force and found himself flying night ground support missions in the first Gulf war. Seventeen missions and a crash landing completed his tour. Shortly after returning to the States, he took a job at Seneca Airlines because he wanted to continue flying, and working for a regional airline meant he could spend more time enjoying the small town life he enjoyed. He had never had the interest nor the time for tomatoes. Flying was just a job to Mike. He raised tomatoes, helped run a scout troop and was a board member of his church. Watching Mike checking the instruments, Jack recognized a strong similarity between Mike and Jack Wilson, Jr. They were both very idealistic or, as Jack Jr. termed it, "involved".

Jack realized Mike had been talking to him and was tugging on his sleeve.

"We're having a small group over Friday. Low key. How about you and Barb joining us?"

"Don't know...something at the school." He really felt he should accept. Mike was always trying. "I'll check with Barbara and let you know." He wouldn't, although he knew Barbara would enjoy an evening at Mike's.

"We'll leave a spot open. Even if you have to come late, we'll have plenty to eat."

He could hear passengers clattering up the boarding stairs. Turning in his seat, he watched them filing out of the terminal with newspapers, magazines and umbrellas over their heads. The constant construction and temporary stairs were a real inconvenience any time but especially when the weather was bad. Jack watched a teenage boy stumble up the stairs and wished he knew his son better. They got along, but it was more a social relationship than a father-son one. It was the same with the girls. He knew his daughters loved him, but they weren't too interested in what he had to say. "You don't understand, Daddy," was a common phrase around the house. Maybe he didn't understand. At least he couldn't understand why his son felt the way he did about....

"Coffee, guys." Amy weaved her way into the cramped cockpit, stepping over chart cases while dodging the overhead switch panel.

"I think you'll have to shake him," Mike said, nodding to his left.

"This will wake you up," she said, wrapping Jack's fingers around the paper cup.

Jack sipped the hot coffee. "Sorry, crew, the Captain is now on board."

The preflight check and engine start were completed and Mike started the taxi to the runway. Jack thought it odd that Mike had more in common with Jack Jr. than he had himself. His son spent a lot of time explaining how he wanted to spend his life doing something important. Jack shook his head not knowing for sure what the phrase meant. Or what his son meant either.

"Seneca 265 hold for landing traffic at runway 28," crackled from the radio. Jack could barely see the twin pencils of light from the approaching airliner's landing lights stabbing the darkness to his left. The plane touched down and glided past them, spewing rooster tails of water behind the wheels. Jack released the brakes and steered the MD-80 onto the runway.

As the landing airliner turned off the other end of the runway, the tower gave clearance for takeoff and Jack slid the throttles forward. The airliner shuddered for a moment and then began rolling, slowly at first, then faster and faster. Jack tensed his fingers on the wheel and licked his dry lips. He knew the takeoff was why he flew. The sensation of immense power, anticipation, even a little fear. After all the years of flying, every takeoff was still like the first. Just past midfield he pulled the wheel back slowly. The plane smoothly left the ground and climbed toward the clouds.

"Gear up."

"Gear up," Mike returned as Jack began a steep turn to the right. "People are different now," Jack mumbled to himself. It wasn't just Jack Jr. and Mike. He didn't understand how, exactly, or why. Maybe....

"Jack!"

He saw the flashing red light just as Mike called out. "Fire in number two engine." Mike's voice had returned to calm. Jack cut fuel to the engine as Mike raised the switch to activate the fire suppressant system. They watched the red warning light flicker, then wink out. Jack wasn't too concerned. There were two engines, one mounted on each side of the tail, and the MD-80 could easily fly with one. He had leveled off at seven hundred feet and now he cautiously started a slow turn back toward the airport.

"Mike, tell everybody what's going on. I'll call the tower."

Before Mike could key the intercom the airliner shook violently, nearly wrenching the wheel from Jack's hand. They hadn't heard a sound, but Jack knew the engine had exploded. He was concerned now. The controls didn't feel right and the whole rear of the plane might be in flames. "Go back and take a look."

Jack keyed the intercom to tell the passengers to make sure their belts were tight, there was nothing to worry about; they had lost an engine but could fly with one.

"Seneca 265 returning with blown engine." Jack radioed.

"Seneca 265 cleared on either runway, your choice. Emergency crews alerted. Please advise intentions."

Mike reentered the cockpit and strapped himself into the seat. "Big holes where pieces of the engine ripped through the tail section but no fire. Amy'll let us know if anything changes. How're the controls?"

"Okay."

"Uh-oh," Mike said softly. They both sensed it at the same instant. Jack pushed the throttle to increase power to the remaining engine. They watched the vibrating tachometer needle begin to slowly drop. Fragments from the exploding engine had damaged the other one. Jack pumped the throttle in a useless attempt to resuscitate the dying engine. The power started to slowly drop; then the MD-80 started to drop too.

"We can't make the airport." Jack's voice was calm but urgent. "We've got to find a place to put it down."

Mike peered out the window into the rain and could barely discern lights below.

"The parkway," Jack said quietly. Mike stared past Jack's face at the parkway about two miles to their left. Even through the rain the mercury-lit strip of concrete was plainly visible.

"We can't!" Mike stared at Jack in disbelief. "Even if we make it that far, what about the people on the highway?"

"Our only chance is the parkway." There was no more time for discussion. Jack completed a tight turn that aligned the airliner with a straight stretch of highway. He began rehearsing the forced landing in his mind: he would land in the lanes where traffic was moving in the same direction. That would ensure that any collisions with cars would be less than head on. There would be a period where the airliner would rapidly overtake cars, but by landing as slow as possible, and by applying brakes hard, he hoped to keep that time to a minimum. With a little luck, there wouldn't be many cars. He had lowered the flaps and was waiting until the last minute to lower the landing gear, keeping airspeed at a maximum to avoid a stall.

"Gear down," Jack ordered. The plane slowed dangerously as the landing gear pushed into the wind. Jack worked the wheel and rudder pedals to trim the MD-80 to the changed flight characteristics. Mike had always been impressed with Jack's skill, but his amazement increased each second. With almost no power in the remaining engine the plane was lined up perfectly with the highway, and they were going to touch down right at the beginning of a straight stretch of concrete. Jack's white fingers tightened on the wheel. His right hand shot out and cut power to the struggling engine. Then, twenty feet above the concrete his blood froze. He saw it but was past the point of having any options. Just as the MD-80 was settling to the highway a large tractor trailer rounded the curve from their right and loomed in front of them. He jammed the rudder pedal hard, yawing the nose to the left, and the right wing slammed into the box trailer with a roar. The plane twisted violently to the right, then skidded to the left, grinding into the medial barrier. The MD-80 slid across the medial strip onto the oncoming lanes of the parkway, spraying large pieces of aluminum behind. Some drivers instinctively drove off the road; those who didn't stabbed their brakes in a futile attempt to avoid the careening airliner. The deafening screech of aluminum sliding on concrete was punctuated by the roar of oncoming cars slamming into the plane. The MD-80 finally slid off the highway, bounced over a shallow embankment and wrenched to a stop in a drainage ditch.

Jack and Mike sat momentarily in the sudden silence listening to the patter of rain on the aluminum skin above their heads. Jack's immediate fear was fire. He jumped to the cockpit door and peered into the cabin. It was too dark to see, but he could hear people moving about. He pulled the emergency lever and kicked the front cabin door open.

"Everyone out. We're okay." Jack was shaking but his voice was steady. "Take it easy; it's a slight drop to the ground." The plane filled with eerie shadows as Mike entered the cabin with a flashlight. Jack noticed Amy helping people out a rear exit. "Easy now, watch your step," he tried to reassure people as he helped them jump to the ground. He was relieved to notice that although there were bloody noses and mouths everyone was walking. "Last one, Mike. Give me the light and get out."

He ran down the aisle checking the seats for stragglers. He yanked open the restroom doors; empty. Jack searched the compartments above the seats as he retraced his steps to the front of the cabin. On one of his flights a mother had placed a small child in a rack to sleep. After checking the cockpit for anyone who might have wandered into it, Jack jumped to the ground. He could see figures on the embankment above scampering like goats up a mountain toward the highway. Some were being helped by others. He sloshed out of the water-filled ditch and began stumbling up the hill. He started to laugh. He had made it! He was laughing so hard he fell to his knees and couldn't get up. Jack finally staggered to his feet and continued climbing up the hill. He had pulled it off! He couldn't be sure yet, but it looked like everyone was okay.

He reached the top of the hill and was met by chaos. Cars were stopped on both sides of the road, horns blaring from under crushed hoods, and lights flashing randomly. Amy ran up to Jack and cupped her hands over his ear to compete with the bedlam.

"Only bloody faces and a broken arm; he got that jumping to the ground."

Jack didn't answer, but the headlight glare reflected the look of satisfaction on his face. He heard a siren and watched a flashing red light approach on the berm. Two state troopers jumped from the car and ran up to them.

"Anyone hurt?" the first trooper called out. Without waiting for an answer the troopers hurried toward a group of passengers to see if anyone needed immediate attention. Jack walked slowly behind them.

"How long till the ambulances get here, Officer? These people are pretty frightened."

Officer Hannah turned to face Jack Wilson. He was over six feet, about fifty, with large teeth that showed through tight lips. The trooper's face was framed by streams of water dripping from his wide brimmed hat.

"Pretty frightened?" Officer Hannah bellowed over the noise from the auto horns. "Some people up the road are pretty hurt. Some dead."

Disgust was clearly evident in Hannah's eyes. For the first time Jack thought about the cars they had hit when landing.

"Johnson," Hannah yelled, "radio we don't need medical personnel here until they're done up the road." The horns gradually stopped as the batteries in the wrecked cars drained or were disconnected. Hannah turned to Jack as Johnson's feet crunched over the gravel toward the patrol car. His face was alternately dim then bright red in the flashing emergency lights. "Why?" Hannah asked slowly, "Why did you land on a highway?"

Jack flushed with anger. Didn't this cop understand? "Don't second guess me! I gambled a few lives to save more than ninety. Looks like I won!"

"You should have landed somewhere else. There are dead people on that highway."

"There would be dead people on that plane otherwise." He glared at the trooper. "They were my responsibility; not the people on your highway." The cop just didn't understand. Jack was thinking of the auto deaths objectively. The trooper would understand eventually, he thought. He was too emotionally involved to realize it now.

Jack was conscious of car horns blaring again as drivers blocked by the wreckage became impatient with the delay. Johnson was running up to the two men.

"How much longer?" Hannah called out.

"We'll have one lane clear in ten minutes," Johnson shouted. "They're dragging that yellow convertible off the road now."

Jack grabbed Hannah's arm and in the glare of the rain dimmed headlights Hannah could see the smug look on Jack's face had changed. Hannah leaned closer and shouted as loud as he could over the impatient din of auto horns; "No need to look so concerned, Captain. She wasn't your responsibility."

Duel Over Lake Michigan

Gayle Patterson rushed down the jetway, her long chestnut hair flying to the side as she rounded the corner and entered the cabin of the MD-80.

"Hi," Ruth Mitchell called out as Gayle slid to a stop in the confined entryway. "It's about time you visited your old friends."

"Hi, Ruth." Gayle smiled sheepishly. She had hosted many flights with Ruth out of Chicago's O'Hare airport. Since she changed jobs she had been too busy to keep in touch. Not much of an excuse, really. "I haven't been seeing much of anybody lately." She squeezed past Ruth and stuck her head into the cockpit. The subdued whine of instruments and electronic equipment always excited her.

"Hello, guys."

Robert Marting and Tom Jessop turned and greeted her, surprised. "Hi, Gayle." Robert's booming voice was almost too loud for the small confines of the cockpit. He glanced at the small satchel in Gayle's hand.

"Curious, aren't you?"

"Well, it's just that when an airline captain sees a security officer on his plane he wonders why."

Robert's feelings concerning the airline security system were well known. He was the vice-president of the Air Line Pilots Association and had recently gained considerable influence with legislators in Washington. He had convinced them that too much emphasis was being placed on preventing terrorists from getting on a plane and not enough to deal with the problems after they were on board. Once a plane was commandeered, Robert insisted that any reasonable demands should be met. He argued that armed guards on planes and the probable shootout could prove to be as homicidal as the terrorists' actions. He also believed the emphasis on foreign terrorists neglected the risk from domestic threats. Bombing of the Murrah Federal Building in Oklahoma City by a decorated Army veteran proved that not all threats are instigated by foreigners.

"I've been in Chicago three years. It's time for a visit home."

"I seem to remember you weren't too fond of home," Tom said, underlining an item on the checklist.

She shrugged her shoulders. "I'm sort of looking forward to it." Turning to leave, she bumped into Ruth who was entering the cabin with a second round of coffees.

"Well, Gayle, decide to come back?"

"No, just another passenger ordering a smooth flight and a good drink as soon as possible after takeoff."

"Talk to Robert about the smooth flight, but we'll be serving right after wheels up," she said helping Gayle back through the door.

Gayle walked to the rear of the cabin. The plane wouldn't be full so she took a seat in the last row in front of the tail boarding stairs so she could talk to Ruth during the flight. She dug into her purse for a comb and mirror. Gayle flicked her head from side to side while combing as feminine women do until satisfied her hair was presentable. She stretched her legs as best she could in the confined area and thought about the new job.

She hadn't really expected them to give a twenty-seven year old stewardess a chance. But who was better qualified? After graduating from her home-town college with a degree in Criminal Justice, she served in the Military Police in the Army including four months in Iraq during the first Iraq war. So, when the airline was upgrading its security force after the World Trade Center attacks she applied for the job of Assistant Deputy for Security. Although the federal Transportation Security Agency had responsibility for screening passengers, the airline wanted to take steps to reduce risks from their own employees and subcontractors. Top management believed a major event at an airline the size of theirs could put them out of business. They became much more aggressive after the incident at their base airport where a disgruntled employee of another airline had "gone postal" and shot two fellow employees and an innocent bystander. She had been on the job now for two years and enjoyed it more every day.

The plane lurched as the tug pushed it back from the terminal building, and one of the engines emitted a small whine as the starting sequence initiated. When Ruth had finished parroting the emergency exit and oxygen mask instructions she sat beside Gayle and buckled up.

"Miss it, Gayle?"

"Nope. Watching you wrestle with the oxygen mask convinced me."

"Anybody aboard we should be worried about?"

"Hey, I'm on vacation. Do you serve coffee, tea and wine on your day off?"

Ruth laughed. "I don't know if you can spot them before they do something anyway. I've seen a lot of weird passengers that didn't turn out to be terrorists or skyjackers. I often wonder though."

Gayle straightened in the seat as the MD-80 began rolling down the runway. "Well, you're aware of the profiling debate aren't you?"

"Yeah, I know that everyone is jumping to behavior profiling to get around the political issue of ethnic profiling. I'm not sure that everyone who appears nervous, or moves erratically can be handcuffed, though. You just can't arrest everyone with a nervous twitch."

"True, but certain behavior should cause suspicion and follow-up questioning that can cause a person who is a real threat to tip their hand."

Gayle always seemed to be justifying the screening procedure. It seemed that most people were either very emotional about ethnic and racial profiling concerns, or opposed to new approaches like behavior profiling that they didn't believe could be effective.

"Don't you get tired of all the false alarms?"

"Nope, it's just like fishing. You have to enjoy fishing even when you don't catch any fish. Actually, my biggest concern is that people can be trained to not exhibit telltale behavior."

"You're turning me into a believer," Ruth said, unbuckling her belt, "but right now the passenger profile indicates they want their drinks."

Gayle settled deeper into the seat and looked out the window. They had just emerged from broken clouds, and diffused moonlight filled the cabin with a pleasant glow. The intercom crackled and she recognized Robert clearing his throat.

"Ladies and gentlemen, this is the captain…"

"My," Gayle said to Ruth tugging at a drawer right behind her in the aft galley. "Doesn't he sound formal tonight?"

"…we have a skyjacker in the cockpit."

Gayle immediately looked up the long aisle and stared at the cockpit door. She hadn't seen or heard anything unusual.

"He has assured us that if his directions are followed no one will be harmed. This is not a terrorist situation. Everyone, including the cabin staff, are to remain in their seats. We will give you more information as soon as we can." The intercom hummed, then went dead.

Ruth sat down excitedly. "Wow!" she said.

"Ruth, how did he get into the cockpit?"

"I don't know. The front cabin crew didn't see anything either."

The intercom buzzed again. "We've been in contact with the ground. Our guest has demanded money and parachutes. We'll land as soon as they are delivered at the airport. He emphasizes that all passengers will be released when we land if there is no trouble. Once again, everyone must remain in their seats."

Good old Robert. Gayle was aware of his reputation for unflappability and his calm commands confirmed it. He seemed in control of a very unpredictable situation.

"What a going home present," she thought. She remembered leaving home because she felt uninvolved in all the excitement that was happening everywhere else in the world.

"Gayle," her father had insisted, "there are plenty of opportunities here."

"Dear," her mother had chimed in, "We always thought you would stay here; not run off as soon as you graduated."

That meant getting married and having kids. She loved her parents, but they were not able to understand. She would never forget the first phone call home to her father. Gayle had arrived in Chicago not knowing anyone and found a job almost immediately.

"An airline stewardess, Gayle?" Long silence. "An airline stewardess." He hadn't even tried to conceal his disappointment.

This was her first visit home since she had left. She hadn't even called; just sent a postcard to let them know she was coming.

The sound of the flaps whirring down broke her trance. "Ruth, why don't you sit up front in case the crew needs something?"

Ruth turned to look at Gayle. She knew her well enough to realize her request concealed something, but also knew it would be futile to ask questions. "Okay. See you later."

She watched Ruth walk to the front of the cabin. The plane was about three fourths full and everyone was watching the cockpit door between sporadic conversations about what might happen next. Gayle rose from her seat slowly and inched toward one of the rear restrooms.

"Slow," she thought, "take your time." She reached behind her back, opened the door, and slipped inside.

The change in engine pitch indicated they were on final approach. Gayle braced herself for the landing. She didn't have a plan yet, but when the plane left with the skyjacker she was going to be on it.

The MD-80 settled to the ground and rolled to the end of the runway. Robert keyed the intercom and reminded everyone to stay seated, and told them to be ready to leave promptly when told to do so. She felt the airliner turn around, taxi to the other end of the runway and turn around again. The engines were left running and the plane was facing into the wind ready for take-off.

"Smooth," she thought. "This guy knows what he's doing." She leaned forward and opened the door slightly. Tom Jessop was barely visible directing someone by the front cabin door. He was sliding a large canvas bag into the forward galley area. Tom started to direct passengers off the plane.

Gayle eased the door closed. She was trying to analyze the situation and figure out what the skyjacker planned. If only she had watched more closely when the passengers were boarding. She gave him credit for unloading the passengers. The pilot and copilot were enough for hostages and would be easier to manage. It was obvious he was executing a well thought out plan and that he knew something about aviation procedures. She hadn't the slightest idea how she was going to trip him up. The lazy engine whine slowly built to a roar and the plane started down the runway. "Well," she thought, "I'll get my chance."

The plane rose from the ground, banked toward Lake Michigan, and leveled off at low altitude. "Looks like he'll jump soon. There must be someone waiting with a boat."

Her ears felt a difference in air pressure as the cockpit door opened. Her blood froze as she realized the skyjacker might search the plane. Her only chance, if she were to get one, depended on surprise. She turned the lever and opened the door slightly seconds before hearing footsteps. The opposite restroom door was pushed open, then closed quickly. Gayle took a deep breath and recoiled against the bulkhead as the shaft of light from the open restroom door widened slightly, then disappeared as the door slammed shut. She released her breath slowly. Who would expect an open door to conceal anyone? "At least I can outsmart him."

She heard a coffee pot bang onto a tray, then silence. She waited long enough for him to return to the cockpit, then carefully opened the door. Gayle peered down the long aisle flanked by empty seats and littered with head pillows. She smiled at the ludicrous sign on the cockpit door. Large red letters proclaimed boldly, AUTHORIZED PERSONNEL ONLY.

Her mind raced frantically; she had to figure out what she was going to do. What could she do? Maybe she could signal Robert through the intercom in the galley area. No, too much chance the skyjacker would notice. His actions so far indicated he had more than a layman's knowledge of aircraft. Her eyes focused again on the cockpit door at the end of the aisle, and an idea started to form.

Gayle stepped from the restroom and closed the door quickly. She ran to the front of the cabin and flattened her back against the bulkhead beside the cockpit door. She would wait until he came out and grab him. She would only have to confine him for a few seconds until Robert or Tom could help.

She rehearsed mentally what she would do. Surprise would give her a decided advantage. Her Military Police training should be more than enough to confine him for the few seconds needed. "He probably has a gun," she thought. She almost panicked when it occurred to her he might have a bomb. Odds were against that, she reasoned. Money and parachutes indicated this guy planned to live. Anyway, she couldn't think of any other options.

Satisfied her plan could work, she leaned back to wait. Her eyes fell on the parachutes a few feet in front of her. Two of them. Were there two skyjackers? How could she handle two? Must be only one, she thought, two or more people couldn't have entered the cockpit without one of the attendants noticing. And Robert had used the singular word "skyjacker" more than once.

Gayle shuddered as she remembered an incident in Chicago. A guy had stopped her in the Loop district one night when she was returning from a late flight. He was a dirty, ugly man with a sick look in his eyes. He walked up to her as though he were going to ask for a handout. Suddenly, he grabbed her coat and pulled her face toward his and dragged her toward an alley. She fought her fear and placed a hand on either side of his head and pushed her thumbs into his eyes. She could still hear her thumbnails breaking and feel the strain of pushing with all her strength. Screaming, he turned to run only to trip over her suitcase.

Just as she was beginning to wonder if she could stand her increasing nervousness, Gayle heard the cockpit door handle rattle. The instrument whine flooded her ears as she tensed, and Tom Jessop entered the cabin. Gayle braced herself to grab the next person through the door; but no one followed. Tom hadn't noticed her flattened against the bulkhead, and he was pulling intently at parachute straps. It seemed that no one else was coming from the cockpit, but the door was still partially open, so she thought it best not to try signaling him. She stood quietly, pressing against the bulkhead as tightly as she could, waiting for him to notice her. Finally, he rose and dragged a parachute behind him to the rear of the plane, placed it in front of the tail exit, and began quickly returning up the aisle. He was only five feet away when he glanced up. His eyes met Gayle's and he froze!

He glanced quickly through the cockpit door, then back at Gayle. His mustache formed a furry cap over his gaping mouth. She placed a finger to her lips. He quickly moved forward, and pushed Gayle back roughly.

"What are you doing here?"

She thought Tom was really showing the strain and hoped he couldn't be heard over the background noise in the cockpit. "Maybe I can help."

He glanced alternately at Gayle and the slowly swinging cockpit door.

"I hid in the restroom. We can work out a plan."

Tom seemed to be calming down as he reached over and gently closed the door. "Look, Gayle, we're in a tough situation. Keep out of sight while I go up front and let Robert know you're aboard."

"But what if…"

"Don't worry; I'll find a way. Just get back in the restroom before he comes back here." He placed a shaking hand on her shoulder. "You're right. We can work something out."

"I was beginning to think you were coming apart."

He smiled tensely. "We've been under a little pressure, Gayle."

Gayle walked quickly down the aisle and waved briefly to Tom as she entered the restroom. At least they knew she was aboard. Robert would think of something. What a contrast between Robert and Tom. She recalled a landing when the control tower accidentally scheduled their plane and an Airbus on intersecting runways. Gayle had watched petrified as the Airbus raced toward them with smoke streaming from its brakes and tires. As she tensed for the collision, a burst of acceleration pushed her into the seat. Instead of braking, Robert had applied full power. They roared through the intersection an instant before the other plane. Just past the intersection, Robert braked hard, applied full reverse power, and brought the plane to a shuddering stop just before rolling off the end of the runway. She had asked Robert how he knew the other pilot wouldn't do the same thing.

"You have to keep glued," he had said.

"Keep glued?"

"Gayle, most people act instinctively when under pressure. People don't think; they react. That makes them predictable."

"You probably forgot where the brake pedals were."

Robert laughed, then became serious. "If you force yourself to think in a tight situation, you'll always out maneuver the other person. There's almost always enough time to think it through."

Gayle was suddenly aware of footsteps outside the restroom.

"Come on out, Gayle."

She started to open the door slowly, but it was abruptly pushed open. She looked to her right at Robert seated on an armrest, his arms folded across his chest. His head moved slowly from side to side, and his captain's hat was so far off center it looked as though it would fall to the floor at any moment.

"Gayle, Gayle, small and frail," he drawled.

She glanced forward and was immediately concerned because of the open cockpit door.

"Don't worry Gayle, Tom's the only one up there."

"What about the skyjacker?" she said, confusion obvious in her voice and in the way she was looking at Robert.

"There is no skyjacker."

Gayle felt an intense flash of fear.

"Gayle," Robert said quietly, "you have jumped into a real barrel of snakes. We're the skyjacker."

"What are you talking about?" She knew exactly what he meant, but she needed time to figure out what to do. Whatever their plans, they didn't include her.

"We're going to carry the money off in our flight bags."

Gayle thought of the parachutes. An empty parachute dropped at night wouldn't be seen by following aircraft and they were too low for radar tracking. When authorities found it in Lake Michigan they would assume the skyjacker rendezvoused with a boat. A plausible assumption with today's hand-held satellite mapping devices that allow locating a geographic position within a few feet.

"That water's freezing. How do you expect the police to believe he could find a boat in the dark before freezing to death?"

"We've radioed that he's taking one of us with him. That ensures two good 'chutes and guarantees we navigate exactly to the coordinates he gives us." Robert leaned forward on the arm of the seat. "Of course, he won't take one of us with him. We won't know that until he jumps though, and we won't be able to tell anyone because he disabled all the radios."

"What about the fact that an interlock prevents the rear stair exit from being opened when the plane is airborne?"

"The investigation will show that the tail exit controls have been tampered with. As you know, being a security person, the constant turnover of low paid ground support personnel is a real problem."

"He threatened to shoot one of us if the plane doesn't continue on course, at slow enough speed for jumping, for at least 30 minutes after he leaves the cockpit," Tom said, joining them. Even the automatic pilot seemed to be conspiring against her. "Since we have no way of knowing when he jumps, we'll fly straight and level for 30 minutes so he won't kill one of us."

"Clever", Gayle said slowly, playing the game to buy time to think. "You fly for 50 miles below radar altitude. Since nobody knows exactly when he jumps, the cops won't be suspicious when they can't find the highjacker or his pickup boat."

"We've considered every possible angle." Tom smiled.

"Except one," Robert said slowly. The way he said it raised the hair on the back of Gayle's neck. He stood up and smoothed the wrinkles from his sharply creased blue trousers. "Come on, Tom, there's something we have to discuss."

Tom cleared his throat. He didn't look at Gayle as he turned to follow Robert to the cockpit. She watched them walk up the aisle methodically searching purses, coats, and seat pockets for cell phones. Hers was one of the first Tom found.

Gayle clenched her fist and involuntarily placed a white knuckle to her mouth. They could solve their problem only one way. The next time they came through that door she knew she would be in serious trouble.

She looked at the parachute in front of her. Jumping was her only chance! She fell to her knees, grabbed the parachute Tom had dropped there, and began randomly pulling at the various straps and buckles. The more she tugged, the more she realized she didn't have the slightest idea of how to use a parachute. She thought of the icy water. Well, she'd probably land near a boat; plenty of them on Lake Michigan.

She tried to concentrate on untangling the straps but could only think of Robert's laughing face. And the icy water. Gayle looked up at the empty cabin. Clothing dangled forlornly from the open luggage racks above the seats. Everyone had vacated the plane in a near panic. Coats, briefcases, even purses had been abandoned. It didn't make sense. "People just don't think."

Gayle sat back on her heels and took a deep breath. Slowly, a bazaar scheme started to form. The more she thought about it, the more workable it seemed. If only she had enough time! She grabbed the parachute and dragged it into the tail emergency exit area.

Gayle had never activated an emergency tail exit in flight, only during flight attendant training simulations. She didn't really know what to expect. They were at low altitude to enable the "skyjacker's" jump, so she knew there would be no danger from rapid decompression or lack of oxygen. Taking a deep breath she grabbed onto the bulkhead with one hand and pulled the emergency release handle with the other. The tail cone flew away with a roar. She held to the bulkhead until sure there was no danger of being pulled out, and then she strained to heave the parachute through the opening. Turning quickly, she ran up the aisle, stepped up onto an arm rest, and climbed into an overhead luggage rack clawing at coats and blankets to cover herself. Then she lay perfectly still.

She listened for Robert or Tom but couldn't hear anything except the roar of the engines and the rushing air from the open tail exit. Then, through a fold in the blankets, she could see someone moving in the aisle below although she couldn't make out who it was or what they were doing. She was sure Robert's inflated ego could only conclude that, even if she survived the parachute drop, she had jumped to a certain death in the icy water. She knew they would rig the other parachute so it would open and then throw it out of the plane. Tom and Robert would leave it up to the police investigators to construct an explanation of the mystery involving the missing off-duty security officer that had tried to foil the skyjacker but had lost her life in the attempt.

She slowly began to feel how frightened she was and suddenly shivered. It took all her concentration to keep her feet from noisily shaking against the overhead rack. With the rear exit open, the temperature in the cabin had dropped significantly. "Keep glued," she kept thinking to herself as the plane continued flying over Lake Michigan to complete the 30 minute time period Robert was flying after breaking the radios to provide the plausible explanation of why the highjacker and his boat wouldn't be found.

Finally, she sensed the plane start a rapid, climbing turn back toward Chicago. "A few more minutes and it'll all be over."

Glow in the Clouds

Rick inched forward in the seat again and squinted, trying to see anything except clouds. It was so dark he couldn't even see the plastic windscreen he was staring through. He glanced quickly at the dimly lit fuel gauges. The two needles were dropping so quickly he could almost see them moving. At this rate the fuel would be gone in a few minutes. He could only hope the leak didn't get worse.

He peered through the windscreen again, unconsciously leaning forward, even though knowing it was useless. It was impossible to see anything. He started wondering why he thought it so important to be home for Christmas. It really wasn't home anyway since the divorce.

He was suddenly aware of his pounding heart and the clammy sweat on his palms as his grip tightened on the control wheel. Rick keyed the radio to update Air Traffic Control of his situation and that he would be making a forced landing.

"Cleveland Center, Cessna 4, 8, 2, Charlie, Bravo."

"Go ahead, 2, Charlie, Bravo".

"I'll be putting it down now." He knew the chance of a successful emergency landing would be much better if he attempted it while the engine was still running. "Fuel's just about gone. Still no break in the clouds."

The controller could only confirm his position, indicate there were no airfields nearby, and remind him that the terrain below was mountainous, wooded, and not very populated. He thanked him even though it wasn't new information; he had flown this route many times when the weather was better.

He had phoned Susan last week knowing the call would initiate the same arguing and feelings of guilt. This time, though, the conversation had ended differently. After a long pause, where both were wondering why they should continue trying to talk, Susan said quietly, "Come home for Christmas."

"Why, Susan? We never get past the arguing stage, even on the phone."

"The kids want to see you."

He knew it wasn't true. The kids were even more confused than he and Susan were. He remembered her slow breathing as she waited for a response. He really wanted to talk coherently with her. He just didn't seem to be able to make it happen. They hung up without him accepting the invitation or declining. He had put off calling her back until he was on his way to the airfield after receiving a call from his mechanic that afternoon.

"The new fuel line came in early today and the fix went smoother than I expected."

"Well, that's an unexpected piece of good news."

"Yeah, it wasn't as hard to modify as I thought it would be. Testing's all complete, the tanks are full, and you're ready to go."

Thanking him for the extra effort, he suddenly felt this was an unexpected Christmas present to be taken advantage of. He had a spontaneous urge to go home for Christmas. A weather check confirmed it would be okay: it would be cloudy because of an unseasonably warm front, but there would be no rain, snow, or high winds. The break in what had been a full week of wind and hard rain seemed a confirming omen for a trip home.

He glanced again at the needles just as they sank onto their stubby "Empty" pegs. He would be lucky if the engine continued to run for five minutes. It no longer made sense waiting for an opening in the clouds. He pulled back the throttle, lowered the flaps an increment, and trimmed the plane to start a slow descent. As the engine slowed to an idle, a faint smell of gasoline filled the cabin. Rick decided to risk the chance of fire because a running engine increased his odds of maneuvering to a safe landing if he was close to the ground when he emerged from the clouds. He knew it wouldn't be easy even if the engine continued to run because of the darkness and tall pine trees waiting below.

Knowing it was meaningless he glanced at the fuel gauges again. Maybe it was because at least he could see them. Staring out the windscreen again, he suddenly snapped his head to the left. Was that a light? He could barely see a dim glow and then it was gone. He intuitively twisted the wheel and stabbed the rudder pedal to turn the plane. The glow became more pronounced in the windscreen, although still dim. It was difficult for him to control his excitement. All he could do was hope

for a lit section of highway, a grouping of stores, or something with some light and enough space to try a landing. He was well aware there was no use speculating. There was no option but to continue to head in the direction of the glow and hope the clouds would break.

The engine continued to run, but every few seconds there was a slight vibration caused by an interruption in the fuel flow. Not much time now, the engine could stop at any second. He would be able to glide but wouldn't be able to maneuver as well to a landing spot if he got the chance to see one.

The glow had disappeared again but he continued in the direction where he had last seen it. A hole! He could see the glow brighter to his right.

"Last chance!" He pushed the throttle full forward and headed for the increasingly brightening light, hoping to get through the hole in the clouds before the engine quit. The opening disappeared again. He gently closed the throttle and continued the descent slowly. He thought he had seen trees just before the clouds closed, but he couldn't tell how high he was above them.

Settling back, he squinted harder in an attempt to see. He knew he would emerge from the clouds in seconds; he just didn't know how close he would

be to the ground. The engine started to cough, but continued to run. There! Then, suddenly, he saw the break in the clouds he had been looking for. He slid beneath the cloud deck, saw the glow of light off to his left, and quickly turned toward it just as the engine sputtered and quit.

A lake! He then thought it couldn't be a lake; there were lights on it. As his eyes adjusted to the view in front of him, he distinguished skaters on a frozen lake to his left about a quarter of a mile away! Banking tighter toward the lake he realized he was pivoting around a church steeple only 100 feet away. Close, but no threat. In fact, it seemed to be pointing him toward the frozen lake.

Completing the turn, Rick leveled the wings and became acutely aware of how quiet the plane was with the engine stopped. He knew from all the practiced emergency landings, it would be close, but felt he would just clear the trees and make the edge of the ice. He noticed for the first time the large bonfire on the edge of the lake, obviously the source of the glow he saw through the clouds. Some skaters heading quickly for the side of the lake were also clearly visible. They had heard his approach before the engine quit, saw the landing light, and quickly concluded a plane in trouble was heading for the only flat spot in the area.

Only a slight whisper of air leaking through the many small holes common in small planes was audible. Just over the last of the trees, he maneuvered to lose altitude. He was finally able to determine he would definitely clear the trees and at least hit relatively flat ground if he came up short of the lake. If he had calculated the glide correctly, he would reach the ice and wouldn't even damage the plane.

Rick pulled back slowly on the wheel to settle softly on the ice, then he sensed the plane slowly drifting to the right. He had never landed on ice before; it was a new experience. He decided to just let the plane drift until it stopped, fearing even slight braking might cause a sudden spin-out and crash if the wing tip were to dip and strike the ice.

When the plane finally stopped, Rick sat motionless enjoying the sense of no pressure compared to the hyper tenseness of the previous few minutes. The temperature in the plane had decreased rapidly after the engine quit and he could feel the cold sweat on his neck and realized his shirt was thoroughly wet also. Taking a deep breath, he opened the door and stepped down from the cabin, promptly slipping to the ice. From his prone position on the lake, he watched silhouettes of people skating from the bonfire toward the plane. As they slid to a stop, someone bent over and helped him up.

"You okay?"

"Yep. Just another perfect landing."

Everyone laughed and began patting his back while they introduced themselves. A woman poured a cup of coffee from a thermos around her neck and pushed it into Rick's shaking hand.

"I'm really lucky I saw your bonfire. I couldn't see anything through the clouds for the last hour."

A tall man with a minister's collar showing through his open jacket looked at Rick intently. "You don't know how lucky." He pointed to the barely visible steep hills surrounding the lake. "Our church hasn't had a night skating party in years. This missionary church has lost so many members because of all the young people moving away, there's very little activity here anymore."

The woman in the pink parka poured more coffee in his cup as he pulled his jacket from the plane. "We were trying to decide what to do for this year's Christmas church function when a guy suggested we have this skating party."

"Who was it? I'd sure like to thank him. In fact, I should probably get him a Christmas present."

"Don't know," the minister said. "It was someone who just dropped into our planning meeting. Never saw him before, and haven't seen him since. Which is unusual because everyone knows everyone around here."

The conversation quickly turned to Rick. "So, how did you end up in a small plane over our lake with no engine?"

As he told about being caught blind in the clouds, and following the faint glow of their bonfire as it faded in and out of view, he became so disarmed by their interest and concern as they peppered him with questions Rick inadvertently commented, "I don't know why I felt so strongly I had to be home for Christmas anyway. I don't really expect an enjoyable visit." Bringing his narrative to a close, Rick noticed the minister staring at him pensively.

"We're only an hour away from town. Why don't you get your things from the plane and I'll drive you there."

"You don't mind? Seems like you'll be missing a great Christmas celebration here."

The minister looked at him even more strangely. "Don't mind at all. I wouldn't pass up this opportunity to see a real Christmas celebration."

For the first time since landing, Rick felt the sadness regarding his home situation return. "I think a celebration is too much to hope for." He looked at the church with its tall, white steeple, the bright bonfire, and the laughing skaters returning to the shining ice. The scene was such a contrast to the situation a short time ago in the dark, cold plane, where he had felt so alone.

"You're just too close to see," the minister said putting his arm around Rick's shoulder as they started toward the parking lot. Reverend Ralph looked knowingly into Rick's confused eyes, thinking of the set of events that brought this stranger to their small, isolated lake. "Christmas is all about hope. And remember, she asked you to come home, didn't she?"

The Wright Way

Years ago there were two brothers, Orville and Wilbur Wright, who were excellent bicycle repairmen. Since there wasn't much money to be made repairing bicycles in those days, the Wrights decided to take in laundry to bolster their income. People from miles around sent their laundry to the brothers to have it done the "Wright" way. Soon the Wright Cleaning Company become very prosperous. As a result, the Wrights gave up their bicycle shop in order to devote full time to the cleaning business. Although they accepted any type of laundry, including socks and red long-johns, the Wrights specialized in blankets.

In their backyard, the Wrights constructed a massive tank which was fifty feet in diameter and ten feet, six inches deep. Dirty blankets were submerged in the tank full of soapy water and were agitated by thirty-five outboard motors which were mounted to the sides of the tank. After the blankets were washed, the Wrights would hang them on a clothesline to dry. To accommodate the terrific volume of business which the Wrights handled, the clothesline was five and three quarters miles long.

Needless to say, the Wrights were quite tired at the end of the day after first carrying hundreds of wet blankets to the line then bringing the dry blankets back to the shop. One night, while relaxing after a particularly tiring day of blanket cleaning, the Wrights had a spectacular idea.

"Hey!" Orville shouted to Wilbur, "why not build a wood framework to lay the blankets on? Then the air would circulate around the blankets and dry them faster."

"A great idea," replied Wilbur. "And we can build a second framework above the lower one so we can dry more blankets in less space!"

The ambitious brothers set to work the next day to construct a blanket dryer. They first built a wooden framework about two feet off the ground.

They then added a second tier six feet above the lower one.

The next day the Wrights hung the wet blankets on the dryer and were very pleased with the results. As expected, the blankets dried much quicker on the dryer than they did on the clothesline. But the Wrights didn't stop there. They constantly added refinements to their invention. For instance, they mounted the dryer on skids which slid on a small track. Whenever it would begin to rain, a weight connected with a cable and pulley was released that pulled the dryer, wet blankets and all, into a protective shed. When it stopped raining, a second weight was activated which returned the dryer to the sunlight.

Soon the Wrights were the most famous blanket dryers in the entire country. Their orders increased to such proportions that the Wrights couldn't handle them all. Then the brothers had another idea!

"Since our cleaning cycle is slowed down by the amount of time required to dry the blankets," said Wilbur, "we must find a way to speed the drying process."

"I have it!" shouted Orville, jumping to his feet. "We can speed the drying by placing two big fans behind the dryer to draw more air over the wet blankets!"

"Fantastic," replied Wilbur.

So the brothers once more set to work. They rigged up a small gasoline engine which turned the two huge fan blades by means of a complicated array of sprockets and bicycle chains. The fans and engine were mounted on the dryer so they could also be retracted into the shed when it rained.

This final improvement to the blanket dryer was highly successful. The brothers were able to easily wash and dry the multitudes of blankets sent to them by their thousands of customers.

One day, while the Wrights were cleaning blankets, a startling event occurred. Very unexpectedly the weight used to pull the dryer out of the shed released. As luck would have it, Orville was standing on the dryer hanging wet blankets over the top tier. For some reason, unexplained even to this day, the weight began to drop faster and faster. Within seconds the blanket dryer was moving along its track at a high rate of speed. Unable to jump off, Orville hung on for dear life.

However, the crash Orville expected did not occur! When the dryer reached the end of the track, it suddenly rose into the air, blankets, fans, Orville, and all. When the dryer returned to earth, some distance from where it had begun its journey, a very excited Wilbur ran up to shake the hand of a very stunned Orville.

The two brothers were quick to take advantage of the knowledge they had discovered. The Wrights built bigger and better blanket dryers. Since the name "blanket dryer" was no longer appropriate for a flying machine, the name was changed to "arrow rain". The early flying machines were so called because local American Indians (there were many at that time, you know) were annoyed by the noisy, smoky contraptions constantly flying over their heads. As a consequence, many of the first airmen were more than annoyed by the storm of arrows the American Indians were constantly shooting at the aircraft to show their displeasure. Through the years, the spelling of "arrow rain" has been so mutilated by news reporters that it barely resembles the original word. One of the earliest changes was from "arrow rain" to "aero plane". The term eventually evolved to the current "airplane".

The work of the Wright brothers was continued by brilliant people all over the globe. The airplane has become so useful to mankind that it is hard to imagine a civilization without aviation. We owe a great debt to two brothers who thought there had to be a better way to dry blankets.

One More Time

"Gear down." The Boeing 737 slowed as the landing gear pushed into the wind. Ron Johnson worked the controls to align the plane with the runway as he slumped even lower into the left seat. Ahead and below he could see the lights outlining the touchdown point. The sequenced runway approach strobe lights looked like balls of lightning rolling ahead of the plane towards the end of the runway. The red glow from the instruments reflected from Ron's eyes and carried his thoughts away. He remembered when he couldn't wait to land and rush home. That seemed like so long ago.

He flexed his fingers on the wheel. It's senseless, he thought. The divorces he knew of were always because of a third person. Neither he nor his wife cared for anyone else. The problem was, they didn't seem to care for each other either. "Marital incompatibility," Jean's lawyer so eloquently put it.

They had tried counseling, consulting their pastor, other things they thought might help. Next week Jean and the kids would be going back to New Mexico to move in with her parents.

Ron focused on the rolling ball of light seeming to beckon him to the runway. He tightened his grip on the wheel as another flash rolled from under the plane and started its journey to the strip of concrete. Ron's eyes narrowed as he fixated more intently on the flashing light. His arms slackened slightly, the wheel imperceptibly slid forward.

"Ron."

Ron was barely aware of his co-pilot's voice.

"Ron! Too low!" Bill was staring out the window. "You're going to scare them to another airline," Bill laughed nodding his head toward the passenger cabin.

Unlike himself, Bill was always so concerned about the passengers. Actually, Bill seemed concerned about everybody. It wasn't as if Ron didn't care. He did care. But nothing seemed to work.

They would get along fine for a while then everything would fall apart again. It was especially bad now that the kids were teenagers. Just one blowup after another. He was always relieved to head out again on another series of overnight flights. He was even volunteering for them now. Jean was probably right about him just running away from the problems. But he hated the arguments and she always seemed to take their side. He found himself going out of his way to avoid conversation; at least there were fewer arguments. He knew Jean and the "professionals" were probably right about that too; he just found it easier not to get into discussions that he knew would end in screaming sessions.

"Talk to them, Ron. Try to understand how they feel." It wasn't just Jean, everyone seemed to put the blame on him. Why couldn't they try to understand him? He expected more too. He had always thought if he could only get through the Gulf war, everything would be okay. He never really planned to be "airbussing" travelers. "Cattle Airways," he often thought keying the mike to tell another faceless load of passengers what the weather was like at the next stop. Bill, on the other hand, enjoyed going out of his way to talk with the paying customers. He had just returned from one of his typical strolls through the cabin so that the kids could talk to a real airline pilot and to thank the little old ladies for flying on his airline.

"Hey, Ron, you really are too low." Ron sensed a slight anxiousness in Bill's voice. He watched another flash start toward the runway. It would be so easy and fast, he thought, sensing the wheel slip a little further.

"You're not the greatest pilot in the world, but those folks in back are relying on you right now." Bill was joking, but it was forced.

Ron's hand quickly grabbed the throttles. He pushed them forward as he pulled back slightly on the wheel. The airliner roared over the airport fence just as the rolling ball of light seemed to disappear into the ground just short of the runway. He pulled the throttles back and settled the plane to the ground. Bumpier than usual, but not enough for the passengers to notice. The engines roared briefly as Ron reversed thrust to slow the plane for the turn to the taxiway.

"Need a place to stay tonight, Ron?" Bill didn't pry, but he knew about the problems and he was glad to help relieve some pressure when he could.

"No. I'm going home."

"Thought you and Jean weren't speaking."

"We weren't." Ron said straightening in the seat. "Until a few minutes ago, we weren't."

Finally at Fifty

The runway slowly rotated into view from my left across the top of the windscreen as I guided the small Cessna trainer through a turn toward the airport. A glance at the empty seat beside me confirmed this was my first solo flight. I had imagined doing this almost the entire fifty years of my life, and now all I could think was, "Can I do it?"

I leveled the wings at the end of the turn to align the plane with the runway rushing up toward me. My throat was so dry it hurt. I had always had an interest in aviation, and had often thought about taking flying lessons, but there were always good reasons not to do it. I would convince myself it was too expensive, or that I'd wait until the next salary increase. A work colleague finally triggered events that resulted in me leaning forward to apply just a little more power to adjust the rate of descent.

"I hear you're a private pilot," I said to Rob who had just been hired at the office.

"Yeah, I own a Cessna 172. Like to go up sometime?"

"Sure," I said. Then I confided that what I would really like to do was learn to fly. As I briefed Rob on his recently assigned project, the conversation periodically drifted back to aviation. As we wound up our work session, he gave me the name and phone number of his flying instructor.

"The instructor is everything. Makes or breaks you as a pilot."

I thanked him, but as I walked away, I already knew I wouldn't follow up. I was already thinking of all the reasons learning to fly wasn't practical.

"Old Navy pilot," Rob called behind me. "He can do anything with an airplane. He's the one the other instructors go to when they want to improve their technique or get new ratings."

Relaxing in the yard the following weekend, I watched a small plane fly overhead and slowly bank toward the airport two miles from my home. As the sound of the engine drifted into the distance, I went into the house to pour another cup of coffee. Spontaneously, I pulled Rob's card from my wallet, and called his instructor's number.

"Hello, I'm out flying now, but leave a message and I'll call you back shortly."

Well, I could still back out; it was only an answering machine. Fifty year old people don't learn to fly, I told myself. I started to review my usual reasons for not following through in the past. But, for the first time, every reason seemed like a hollow excuse. I mentioned to my wife that I had actually called a flying instructor and left a message. I repeated how expensive flying would be.

"Well, you know, we made the last college tuition payment last month," she said. Just as the phone rang, she challenged with, "If you don't spend it, I will."

It was Rob's instructor. After a brief conversation with Bill he gave me directions to the hanger and said he'd see me at three o'clock.

After an introductory handshake, Bill turned and motioned for me to follow him onto the flight ramp and toward a single engine, two seat Cessna trainer. I had flown thousands of commercial airliner miles on business and vacation, but this plane seemed so small; even fragile. It looked like it was made of aluminum foil.

"Go ahead and preflight it," Bill said.

"I told you, I've never done this before. I don't know how."

"Lesson number one. Always use the checklist. You'll find it under the left, front seat."

I walked around the plane, performing the tasks described on the checklist, to make sure the plane was safe for flight. Bill explained each item in detail taking the time to make sure I understood each step of the procedure.

"Never trust small aircraft fuel gauges," he barked up from the ground to me on the wing step as I removed the fuel cap on the top of the wing and inserted my finger into the gas tank to make sure it was full. "They're notoriously inaccurate and you can't just pull to the side of the road and walk to a gas station for a gallon of gas." As I started to step down he placed his hand on my foot on the wing strut step to halt me before I jumped to the ground. "And make sure you screw it on tight. If it vibrates loose in flight, the slipstream will siphon the tank dry before you can get back to the airport."

Not much of a bedside manner, I thought, but he seemed knowledgeable.

It was happening too fast I thought, taxiing toward the runway weaving from side to side because of my inability to move the rudder pedals smoothly. I certainly had not expected to climb into the left seat, start the engine, and actually guide the plane onto the runway as part of the first lesson. I assumed there would be classroom instruction first.

"The best way to learn to fly, is to fly," Bill said.

I steered onto the runway, stretching to peer over the nose, my legs clumsily pushing the rudder pedals to get the plane pointed straight down the runway. I had never seen a runway head-on before. It seemed to extend all the way to the horizon.

"Cessna one, four, delta, cleared for takeoff," crackled from the radio.

"Okay," Bill said, pointing at the throttle. "Let's go."

This guy is really pushing it, I thought. There he sat, calmly, arms folded across his chest. He had only known me twenty minutes and he was nodding his head to indicate we should be moving down the runway. I dug my fingernails into my left palm as I gripped the wheel tighter and pushed the throttle forward timidly with my right hand. As the engine roared and the plane lurched forward, I thought that he should at least unfold his arms and be ready to grab the wheel, or something.

"Keep your hand on the throttle," Bill shouted over the noise. "You don't want it to vibrate away from the full power position, and sometimes you have to cut the engine quickly if a takeoff has to be aborted."

"Now! Bring the wheel back. Slowly. That's enough, hold it there."

After all the years imagining what it would be like, I actually sensed the force of the air pushing back against the wheel as I pulled it toward me. Suddenly, the side to side gyrations of the plane and the vibrations abruptly stopped, and the pounding noise turned into a smooth hum. The plane was climbing effortlessly into the air. What had been a flimsy machine on the ground felt solid, secure, and natural in its element. I slowly realized I was breathless and thrilled. I knew at that point that nothing would ever be the same.

"Push the wheel to drop the nose a little to increase the airspeed to seventy knots. You don't want to stall this close to the ground."

During that takeoff, flying changed from something I had always wanted to do to something I had to do. At the end of that first lesson, I signed up for the private pilot course.

An unforgettable event when learning to fly is the first time a student pilot flies the plane without the instructor. Every novice pilot anticipates the first solo flight with some trepidation and most initial instruction is focused on that event. You want to do it, but you're not sure you can. As you approach the eight hours of dual instruction, the minimum amount of training time legally required before a student can fly alone, you realize how much you still have to learn. You actually relax a little because you feel you're not quite ready and it won't happen for another few lessons. That's why it always comes as a total surprise.

"Pull over to the ramp," Bill said after I had bounced the plane to a far from perfect landing at a small airport where we practiced because there was less traffic. I thought we would taxi to the airport café to discuss technique over a coffee as we often did when my progress had hit a plateau.

"I'm getting out and you're not," Bill said as he cracked the door and put a foot out onto the ramp. "That okay with you?"

He had twisted in the seat to stare straight into my eyes. I'm not ready, I thought, and felt a sudden surge of panic! It's unbelievable how completely a student pilot eventually trusts his instructor's skill and judgment. It's similar to a confessor relationship.

In certain respects, Bill knew more about me than my parents and wife.

"If you think I'm ready, I'm ready."

He closed the door and slowly walked away. I looked for an encouraging wave, but he didn't even look back.

"Just fly around the airport once and land. Most people get too excited to do any more safely," he had said as he stepped out.

"Rostraver traffic," I muttered into the microphone as I reached the end of the runway. "Cessna one, four, delta entering runway two, six for takeoff."

The first solo takeoff was so different. Without Bill's weight the small plane leaped forward and seemed to jump into the air. Passing low over the highway at the end of the runway, I could clearly see the drivers' faces through the car windshields. The Monongahela river burst into view at the bottom of the 300 foot bluff on the other side of the road. I glanced repeatedly at the empty seat beside me. I had never felt so alone.

"Level off to build up airspeed." Bill wasn't there, but I could hear his voice. "Now, a gentle turn to the left. Keep the airspeed at 75 knots but don't let the engine overheat."

Completing a second turn that sent me back toward the airport I started to feel I could pull it off. Flying parallel to the runway I had just left, but in the opposite direction, I suddenly remembered it was time to start planning the landing.

As exciting as takeoffs are, landings are even more so. There are so many things that have to be done, and so many ways to do them wrong. The appropriate increment of flaps has to be selected at the proper time, engine speed has to be set correctly, trim adjusted, and carburetor heat turned on. There was no concern for personal safety, only the dread I would embarrass myself by damaging the plane, or worse, contradict the confidence Bill had shown in me when he stepped out of the plane. After all, his instructor's license and reputation were on the line.

I worked the controls gently to fine tune the plane's descent to the runway, seriously wondering if I could do it. The repetitive glances at the right seat, and the empty seat belt on it, confirmed that I would have to do it. As the plane got closer to the ground, my thoughts turned from wondering whether I could do it, to whether I could do it well.

"It's easy to make a safe landing," I could hear Bill saying. "It takes skill to make a good one."

Cutting the throttle back all the way as the plane passed over the airport fence, I gently pulled back the wheel, then pulled harder when about five feet above the ground. The Cessna slowly settled to the runway, without bouncing, and with almost no noise from the tires. Not perfect, but pretty good! I eased the wheel forward, to settle the nose wheel slowly to the ground. I can't explain the sensation I felt at that moment, but I will remember it always.

As the plane slowly rolled toward a stop, I realized I had done it. Finally, at fifty years of age, I had piloted a plane.

As important as that day was, it was only one of many milestones passed acquiring the private pilot's license. Amazingly, every flight is just as exciting as that first solo because there's always something unanticipated and new to discover. An unexpected bonus is that much of the knowledge I have gained has nothing to do with flying.

Desert Synergy

Bob Johns turned a sharp curve on the road winding up to the airport and braked to a sudden stop as he recognized the vehicle he had just passed was a police Jeep. He backed up as he lowered the passenger-side window.

"I'm looking for the sightseeing pilot with the open plane. Can you tell me where to find him?"

"Sure. Let me check to see if he's there."

Bob could hear the radio crackling but couldn't make out the words.

"Follow me. It's just at the top of the hill."

Nothing like a police escort Bob thought following the Jeep to the top of the plateau 500 feet above Sedona. Not only were the red rocks and hills beautiful, the people were friendly. By the time he parked and removed the camera equipment from the trunk, the cop was already talking to a rugged faced guy in jeans and a shirt embroidered with Native American symbols.

"Looking for a pilot?" Adam Kotori said offering his hand to Bob.

"Yeah, I hear you have an open plane so I can get some good pictures."

"It's open, all right. How about giving me a hand rolling it out."

As the large overhead hanger door rose, Bob was able to barely make out a large wooden propeller and round nose cowling filled with engine in the dark shade of the hanger.

"Grab there and push with me."

Bob stepped back when they were finished and looked at the biplane. It was big, and bright yellow, every inch of its large metal nose and fabric covered wings, fuselage and tail. Bob had to squint to look at it in the bright morning sun.

"What you want to take pictures of?" Adam said wiping his hands on a rag.

"Would like to get some aerial shots of one of the Sanaguan cliff dwellings, one about twenty miles west of here." After a pause Bob added, "If you don't mind," unexpectedly feeling a need to be sensitive to the pilot's obvious Native American heritage.

"I know the one you mean, and I don't mind at all," Adam smiled. "I appreciate what they represent but it isn't a religion with me. In fact, I like to see other people show interest in them. Plane's already fueled. Give me ten minutes to preflight it and we'll be gone." As Adam started toward the plane he turned. "How about some coffee?"

"Already got it," the cop said emerging from a small office inside the hanger carrying three cups and an old metal coffee pot. "Adam's hospitality isn't always the best," he said filling Bob's cup.

"Bob, this is Sheriff Will Abner. He starts a lot of his mornings up here drinking my coffee."

"Well, guess I'll watch your takeoff from the valley. Gotta get back to work."

"Work? Who you trying to kid?" Adam returned.

"You'd be surprised. We don't all have fun jobs," the sheriff called back as he climbed into the Jeep.

Adam handed Bob a pair of goggles and a headset, then pointed to the safe places to step on the wing to climb into the forward cockpit. Adam helped him adjust the seat and strap in, then climbed into the rear cockpit. After a few minutes, the propeller started to turn slowly and the engine started with a shudder and a roar, throwing blue plumes of smoke back over the plane. Adam waggled the ailerons, elevators and rudder as he revved the throttle to move the plane onto the taxiway. He weaved the plane from side to side as they rolled down the tarmac because of the impossibility of seeing over the up-tilted nose when the plane was sitting on the tail wheel.

They stopped at the end of the taxiway as Adam pushed hard on the brakes and revved the engine to a high pitch to check the magnetos, oil pressure, engine temperature and other items critical for flight. Looking out over the valley, Bob understood why Sedona airport is referred to as the "aircraft carrier of the desert". The top of the high mesa had been leveled for the runway and it stretches from one end of the mesa to the other. When planes rise from the runway they're already 500 feet in the air. He was trying to prepare his cameras but couldn't help being distracted by Adam's preparations to fly.

He didn't know much about planes, but he could tell this one was special. He watched the control cables moving through openings in the floor and side panels and sensed the immense power in the engine now slowing to an idle with a rhythmic loping rumble as Adam completed the flight checks. His comment over the intercom was met with "She's special, alright. A 1932 Waco. Not a reproduction either; the real thing. Did a lot of the restoration myself." The pride was obvious and the pilot's voice also showed the excitement of flying the vintage plane.

The earphones clicked as Adam keyed the radio. "Sedona traffic, Echo, 4,7, Nancy taking runway 0,3; departing to the west."

"Okay, Mr. Tourist, here we go."

The plane turned onto the runway and before the turn was completed, Bob watched the dual-throttle slide slowly forward followed by a roar and a blast of heat off the engine. The plane quickly lifted off the tail wheel as it gained speed and Bob could see the onrushing runway through the spinning propeller. Hardly off the runway, Adam banked sharply to the left. The ground dropped away quickly because of the plane's steep climb and the airport's high altitude off the valley floor. He listened to the strumming of the wires supporting the wings as the plane leveled off and the engine noise decreased. Adam had asked him if he was a "conservative" or a "fun" flyer. He had opted for "fun".

Adam called his attention to some elk running below. "Used to be a lot of them, but not anymore. They'll probably all be gone in five years."

Bob could remember when Sedona was mostly red rocks and scrub. Now residents were seriously concerned about whether enough water was going to be available in the near future.

"Never had a request to view that particular ruin before. It's pretty inaccessible and off the normal tourist path. Looking for anything in particular?"

"No. Don't need to get too close." Bob was still concerned about how Adam felt flying him to the site. " Just thought I saw some movement up there yesterday. Probably my imagination."

"Really, no need to be so sensitive. Actually, I've meant to learn more about the cliff-dwellings for a long time. My parents talked about them a lot but when you're young you're not interested in what your parents think. Sometimes, the urge to find out more is pretty strong, but I just haven't found the time."

Realizing a lens he had selected before the flight wasn't quite right for the light, Bob switched to a different one and adjusted the camera settings.

He didn't want to go to all this effort only to get average images.

"There it is," squawked through the headset.

Bob peered through the propeller into the morning haze ahead. He looked through the camera's telephoto lens at the slit of the cave-like hollow in the cliff side. The Senaguans dominated the area with a sophisticated society about 700 years ago and then vanished without a trace, leaving behind dozens of cliff dwellings like the one ahead.

"We'll circle around from the south to give you a clear shot over the left side of the plane, and I'll yaw it to the right so the wings will be out of the way. You'll have a clear view."

Bob saw the aileron on the right wing drop down as the plane banked to the left. "Sounds good." As Bob adjusted the camera settings for the light and distance, his attention was unexpectedly drawn to the instrument panel. A green image of Kokopelli was wildly gyrating back and forth inside the round glass of one of the instruments.

"Adam, I'm no aviation expert, but there's a gauge up here with Kokopelli dancing around inside, and that seems a little unusual."

The myth of Kokopelli was one of the reasons Bob found Sedona fascinating. Images of the American Indian symbol have been traced back

3,000 years in the high plains and deserts of the American Southwest and the legend persists to this day. Supposedly the mischievous god of fertility, Kokopelli is often depicted as a humpbacked flute player with a large feathered headdress.

The laugh from the rear cockpit was almost loud enough to hear without the headset.

"That's the omni-directional range indicator. It's used for radio navigation. Don't worry about it; it only acts erratically around this site, and we don't need it on a sunny day. Mine has it too. I think my instrument tech is a comedian. I noticed them after the last time he checked and calibrated the instruments. He denies having anything to do with it even after I called him back to fix them. Unfortunately, I couldn't be there on his return trip and he denies there's a Kokopelli and swears the instruments operate normally."

"Guess its gremlins," Bob offered.

Adam laughed again. "Nope. These instruments are notoriously reliable and their normal behavior is nothing like what you're seeing. It's not gremlins, but I don't have another explanation."

As they flew past the cliff dwelling Bob started taking pictures, varying the camera settings to increase the odds of getting some great pictures. Just as they were flying out of camera range, he thought he saw something unusual through the telephoto lens. "Would you mind going back a little closer? I'm sure I saw something move inside one of the pueblos."

"Sure," Adam returned. "And I have a surprise for you. A bright spotlight I use for night elk spotting. It'll light up the inside of that place like daylight."

"Maybe we'll see some gremlins." Bob shifted the cameras to the rolled leather lip on the other side of the cockpit as Adam healed the biplane over into a steep left bank toward the mesa to get closer for the next fly-by.

Bob was focusing the lens just as Adam fired up the search light and aimed it into the dark slit in the side of the cliff. Just as he thought he could make out what appeared to be piles of knapsacks all over the interior, he saw small flashes of light immediately followed by whistling and loud ripping sounds from the plane. Adam was quicker than he was. As Bob was coming to the realization they were being shot at, Adam had already tossed the plane into a steep left, descending turn.

Before he could ask Adam what was going on, Bob heard a series of heavy thuds followed by a loud bang from the engine, then almost total silence.

He was suddenly aware how close they were to the ground.

"Guess you know by now we're being shot at. Killed the engine."

"Can you get us down okay?"

"That's no problem. The problem is that Humvee paralleling on the right. Whoever's shooting must be in touch with them by radio. I'll get us down okay, but that Humvee might be waiting for us when we land."

Bob looked at the barren desert ahead. Maybe Adam wasn't concerned about a landing with no power but he sure was. He looked down at the Humvee that was having no trouble keeping up with the gliding biplane. Actually, they were so low he was looking over at the Humvee bouncing over the rocks, not down.

"Bob, we don't have many options. When we get on the ground, run. Those guys will get there almost as soon as we do."

Bob pulled the cameras from around his neck. He was aware of the plane dropping quickly at a 45 degree angle to their direction of flight, with the left wing lowered steeply toward the ground. The Waco was in a forward slip, a technique that enables a pilot to lose altitude very quickly. Given another situation Bob would have been impressed with Adam's flying skills but right now all he could think of was the Humvee that had dropped out of sight behind them. He couldn't understand why Adam was throwing away altitude; it seemed like the only thing in their favor. They were only about 10 feet off the ground, at what seemed an alarming rate of speed, and Bob was bracing for the crash that seemed imminent.

"Hang on, Bob! I'm going to try something that might not work, but we don't want those guys to get close to us."

He couldn't see the Humvee, but Bob knew it was right behind them on the desert floor. Just in front of them, Bob saw the ground suddenly rise up just as Adam put the Waco into a steep climb that seemed much too steep that close to the ground. Then, as they passed over a deep arroyo, Adam pushed the nose over quickly just avoiding the stall that would have thrown them into the arroyo nose first. Immediately, the wheels hit the ground on the other side of the arroyo followed by a jolt as the undercarriage collapsed and the plane began sliding on its belly.

Bob was pretty sure the Humvee would be stopped by the arroyo which would give them more time to hide. That is if they survived the crash. The plane was sliding sideways, bouncing over rocks and scrub brush. Bob winced as thorny branches whipped across his face. The plane lurched abruptly to the right and stopped suddenly in a thicket of cactus and thorn bushes.

"You okay?" Adam hollered over the back of the cockpit. "Let's get moving. We have to hide, quick."

He jumped to the ground and ran after Adam scarcely feeling the sharp thorns ripping at his face and body. Adam was waving him toward a large pile of red boulders. "Let's get in there! Quick!"

"Don't know what good that will do."

"We only need to buy some time," Adam wheezed between deep breaths. I got Will on the radio. His guys are on the way."

As they lay quietly, listening for approaching footsteps, Adam's cell phone bleated loudly. "Damn!" he whispered grabbing the phone to silence it. Recognizing the caller number, he flipped it open quickly.

"I guess you're okay if you're answering your cell phone." It was Will. "I was worried because your plane doesn't look too good."

"What about the guys in the truck. They were awfully close."

"It's okay. They were a little slow picking up on your trick. They're at the bottom of the arroyo saying hello to some of my guys."

"We almost were too."

"Yeah. You really ought to learn to fly someday."

Bob and Adam climbed from under the boulders and waved to the sheriff across the arroyo.

"You flushed out some druggies we've been looking for. Sit tight and I'll pick you up in about an hour."

Bob realized he and Adam were scratched up pretty badly as he slowly became aware of the pain. He knew it could have been a lot worse. "Too bad about the Waco. Sure was a nice plane."

"Still nice," Adam said, the disappointment obvious. "She'll fly again. These things are tough. Nothing built today will be flying when they're over seventy years old."

Bob followed Adam as he walked along the plane assessing the damage, slowly moving his hand along the yellow canvas where it wasn't torn. Bob bent over to pick up a camera that had fallen out of the plane when he climbed out in such a hurry. He picked it up and was amazed that it seemed okay. "Hey!" he said jumping up on the lower wing.

"If you don't mind I'm going to get a picture of Kokopelli on that gauge. It'll be a nice souvenir."

Adam just nodded as he continued examining the plane. As he finished his evaluation he returned to find Bob with a perplexed look on his face. "Get your Kokopelli?"

"It's really strange. There is no Kokopelli. I checked in the rear cockpit too. The instruments aren't damaged, so the image couldn't have fallen out."

"Has to be there," Adam said climbing up into the cockpit. "You were probably looking at the wrong instruments. They all look the same to non-pilots."

Bob readied his camera figuring Adam was right.

"That is really strange," Adam said jumping down from the wing, the look on his face clearly indicating puzzlement.

"I was watching it bouncing around like it was alive just before you turned on the searchlight. I know it was there."

"They were there alright. I don't imagine things like that. C'mon, here's our ride," Adam said pointing to the Jeep weaving toward them through the scrub.

Bob looked at the shadowy cliff dwelling set in the mesa off in the distance, then back at the plane. He couldn't help but smile as he thought of the wildly gyrating Kokopelli. He knew he couldn't just walk away.

"Hey, Adam. How would you like to learn more about what your parents were trying to pass on to you? You've got some time now."